PORTFOLIO G

METROPOLITAN SEMINARS IN ART

Great Periods in Painting

PORTFOLIO G

The World Dividing: THE 18TH CENTURY

BY JOHN CANADAY

ART EDITOR AND CRITIC
THE NEW YORK TIMES

THE METROPOLITAN MUSEUM OF ART

THE WORLD DIVIDING

The 18th Century

THE GREAT complex of architecture, painting, sculpture, gardens, fountains, and forest that made up Versailles was a symbol of totalitarian power. It was also the apotheosis of baroque art in some of the aspects discussed in the previous portfolio. In addition, it had a political reason for being: it was a royal domain where Louis XIV gathered together the aristocrats of France to keep them under his watchful eye. Hundreds of people were in residence at Versailles because the king wanted to know what they were doing. Louis's conviction that he ruled by divine right and his thirst for absolute authority reduced the court to impotence. Their days were filled with whatever activities it suited the king to dictate. Expensive pleasures had been included, but toward the end of the old man's reign the life at Versailles became increasingly dreary. Thanks to Louis's overweening ambition, France had alienated the sympathies of Europe. Wars had brought the country to the edge of bankruptcy—a condition to which the construction of Versailles had contributed significantly—and the king had secretly married Madame de Maintenon, who had been governess of his children. Under her influence the court was expected to observe bourgeois standards of morality and a way of life appropriate to the precarious financial situation. None of this was at all to the liking of the spoiled courtiers.

It began to seem to the bored aristocracy that the old man would never die. When at last he did, in 1715, he was close to eighty years old, and there was hardly a person alive who could remember a time when he had not been king of France. He was succeeded not by a son, or even a grandson, but by his great-grandson, who was born at Versailles five years before Louis's death.

The first regent for the boy-king Louis XV was Philippe II d'Orléans, an intelligent but corrupt man. Under Orléans and his successors, and then under Louis XV himself when he came of age, Versailles was the center of a way of life more elaborate, more artificial, more vain, more indulgent, more pleasure-thirsty, and more expensive than any the world had ever seen staged on such a large scale. Things were being carried to even greater extremes when Louis XV, after a long reign, was succeeded by his pathetic son Louis XVI and his queen, Marie Antoinette, both of whom were to die under the blade of the guillotine.

Socially and economically, the life at Versailles was reprehensible, beyond defense of the faintest kind. It delivered the *coup de grâce* to whatever chance France might have had to recover from the plight Louis XIV had created. Historians usually judge Louis XV a wastrel, but some are beginning to defend him as a sovereign who paid attention to his duties. Nevertheless, it is still true that the resources of France were poured into Versailles to support a handful of privileged individuals who were, as useless and selfish as they were, frequently charming and cultivated. They fought bore-

Courtesy of the Board of Trustees for the National Galleries of Scotland

Figure 1

dom in a cycle of fashion, gossip, and love-making, spending millions on trinkets while the common men of France struggled for bread and the bourgeoisie, even when prosperous, chafed under taxes.

The violence of the French revolution that ended this regime, the horror of severed heads carried on pikes, the sadism of mass executions, including (to select a frightful detail that occurred more than once) drinking blood from the truncated bodies of the most hated victims of the guillotine—these excesses can be explained when we understand the excesses and abuses they terminated. Nothing can mitigate the stupidity of these abuses. But art, as it has a way of doing, has preserved for us the ideals of taste that were the saving grace, if not the justification, of the Versailles way of life.

At its best, this way was dedicated to the cultivation of sensibilities, the love of beautiful objects, of nuance, of subtleties. It produced great conversationalists as well as trifling gossips, some of the most exquisite refinements of style, and remarkably few blatant vulgarities.

Esthetically, eighteenth-century court art was the culmination of a thoroughly French tradition. In France more than in any other country, women have from time to time influenced policy and dictated taste. Never was this so true as during the reign of Louis XV. Among the scores of women who served him as pleasures, the official mistresses were not only consorts but arbiters of style. The most influential woman of the time was Madame de Pompadour, the official mistress at the century's apogee. Fortunately for the arts, she was a woman of cultivation and discernment. And, just as in the preceding century the old king and his minister Colbert had set about creating a French art that would be the measure of the power and grandeur of the reign, Madame de Pompadour patronized an art that declared the power of woman, the feminine domination of an age. It was an art of finesse, of intimate refinements, of delicacy, and always of amorous overtones, even when not directly concerned with the glorification of dalliance.

And just as the old king had found in Le Brun the perfect painter to supervise his grandiose projects, Madame de Pompadour recognized in François Boucher (1703–1770) the ready-made stylist for her needs. Boucher, a practical-minded man of simple origins, made his first success as a decorative painter. But he also had great organizational ability for conceiving, executing, or supervising decorative plans and for the hardheaded business of management. He was appointed to the lucrative directorship of the Gobelins tapestry works, among other posts. There was hardly a phase of art and decoration in France that was not to some degree controlled by him.

Under Madame de Pompadour's patronage the tapestry works, the great porcelain makers, weavers of fabrics, cabinetmakers, decorators, architects, and painters flourished. The building and decorating of her own châteaux were enough to support armies of fine craftsmen; in addition, she set a standard for others to follow in a world where fashionable living and competitive display were a premise of existence. In Boucher's portraits of her, Madame de Pompadour (*Figure 1*) is often surrounded by symbols of the intellectual arts that she patronized and, in a small way, tried to practice. Boucher found time to give her painting

Alinari

Figure 2

lessons, but her skill in that area is in doubt.

Between Madame de Pompadour and the painter there was a similarity that, no doubt, she recognized only subconsciously if at all; nevertheless, he was her perfect parallel. Boucher's subjects, like *The Bath of Diana* (*Figure 2*) and *The Toilet of Venus* (Portfolio 11, Plate 127), one of a set of decorations for Madame de Pompadour's luxurious bathroom in the Château de Bellevue, deal with the delights of love. They describe the alluring surfaces of budding youth, the feminine trumpery of laces, ribbons, satins, taffetas, and pretty jewels, the delicate manners and intricate contrivances of the game of love as played under eighteenth-century rules. This was the atmosphere that Madame de Pompadour created around herself for the delectation of the king. It was a constant reminder of her presence, an art of the boudoir and the intimate salon with their promised delights, tender yieldings, coquetry, and sweet excitements. Boucher's painting creates this atmosphere—yet he is a cold painter. His is the art of a consummate stylist and technician, not that of a sensualist. And Madame de Pompadour too was cold. She had one ambition in life, to become the official mistress of the king. Once she achieved it, she set about making herself indispensable. By the time the king's ardor had cooled—or rather, had been redirected—Madame de Pompadour was indispensable indeed. She influenced political policy (disastrously, more often than not) and supervised the king's personal life to assure that the horrid specter of boredom should be kept at bay.

Bildarchiv Foto Marburg

Figure 3

The Rococo

The stage setting for Madame de Pompadour, the style called Louis XV and its more fanciful variations called rococo, is a kind of domesticated baroque. The great rolling baroque forms become gracious curves and curls. In the baroque ceiling illustrating *The Glorification of the Company of Jesus* (Portfolio F, *Figure 3*), gargantuan architecture towered into the sky and figures surged upward toward the revelation of the Holy Trinity. The rococo ceiling in the Prince-Bishop's residence at Würzburg, *Apollo Conducting Beatrice of Burgundy to Barbarossa* (*Figure 3*), by Giovanni Battista Tiepolo (1696–1770), is bound by delicate gold traceries that curl into a sky where cupids fly about in search of likely victims for their darts of love.

Looking back, we can trace the transition from baroque to rococo values in the work of the Coypel family, which constituted something of a dynasty in official French painting. The father, Noël Coypel (1628–1707), was a man of the seventeenth century. He was a lifelong follower of Le Brun, faithful to the Poussinist tradition that Le Brun established as the dominating one of the Royal Academy. As a reward, Coypel was made director of the Academy's branch in Rome, an institution for training young French painters, who competed intensely for the privilege of going there (and who still do so today). Antoine Coypel (1661–1722), who was a youthful prodigy, at the age of eleven accompanied his father to Rome; on his return to France, at only nineteen, he pursued a successful career filled with official commissions and became, in his turn, director of the French Academy in Rome. But he, differing from his father, leaned toward the

Rubensians, who became increasingly powerful in the Academy after the death of Le Brun. His sympathies were shared by his much younger half-brother, Noël Nicolas (1690–1734). Alone among the Coypels, Noël Nicolas was a quiet, retiring fellow; it remained for his nephew, Charles Antoine Coypel (1694–1752), only four years younger, to become the third generation to direct the Academy in Rome. Between them, Charles Antoine and Noël Nicolas completed the transition from Poussinesque baroque grandeur to eighteenth-century style.

Seen side by side with Poussin's *Triumph of Neptune and Amphitrite* (Plate F11), Noël Nicolas Coypel's *Rape of Europa* (Plate G1) tells its own story of the change. In spite of the difference in subject, the same elements—sea, sky, mythical animals and figures with their attendants, and even the arc of fluttering drapery over the central female figure—allow the closest kind of comparison. The eighteenth-century picture is vivacious, whereas Poussin's is static; the Coypel composition dances from figure to figure, leading us in the liveliest way from detail to entrancing detail of a hundred diversionary actions; the Poussin holds each item within a more obviously arbitrary scheme. The Poussin satisfies us by its ultimate effect of order; it is a picture that can best be enjoyed through contemplation. The Coypel seeks not so much to satisfy as to attract, not so much to put details into final order as to make each one interesting, as if the painter feared we might lose interest if any part of the picture remained quiet, as if there were danger of boredom in static balance, as if possibly the observer had not the time for contemplation or the interest in philosophical speculation that is satisfied by the orderliness of the Poussin. Hence he creates a wider variety of more active forms; he heightens his color and applies it more richly, freeing his brush in an accent here and a flourish there, as Rubens did, but in the service of a more superficial ideal.

The comparison sounds unflattering to the Coypel painting and, by inference, to the new century. In a way it is. But *The Rape of Europa* may be enjoyed for something more than its surface charms. If it is less thoughtful in spirit than *The Triumph of Neptune and Amphitrite*, it is nevertheless a superb bit of calculated craftsmanship. Beneath its freedom and variety, the composition is controlled and balanced. The enjoyment of eighteenth-century art—its furniture and decoration, as well as its painting—is not complete if we accept only its face values of lightness, gaiety, and charm. It was an age where consummate skill was frequently applied to trivialities; the lightness and delicacy of its art comes from absolute control of extremely demanding means of creation. This fact must be remembered before the trivialities are dismissed.

The Rape of Europa affords other comparisons, particularly with the three other versions of the subject we have seen, Francesco di Giorgio's (Plate D9), Titian's (Plate E5), and Veronese's (Plate E6).

The Titian and the Coypel are both based on sensuous appeal, but the Titian is more vigorous, more masculine. Its harmonies are bolder, wider, deeper, and fuller. The princess is abducted through a world of glowing light, a world in which sensuousness is the basis of human experience of the most meaningful kind. Coypel's version deals with more silken, more immediate pleasures; it reduces Titian's light-filled universe to an operatic stage offering a delightful production by an expert in stagecraft. We made something of the same comparison between the Titian and Veronese, saying that Veronese's abduction took place decorously, with the polite formality of a court function or a reception for a visiting potentate. If, in turn, we compare the Veronese and the Coypel, we see that the life of the court no longer takes place in grand halls, so to speak, but in intimate drawing rooms. As an adjunct to an eighteenth-century interior, the Titian would have been shattering, overpowering; the

Veronese would have been merely out of scale, a little heavy. The Coypel suits its time because it is delightful, engaging, freshly ornamental, rather feminine in its suggestion, and, we might even argue, deliberately concerned with superficial delights. For delving beneath the surface might be dangerous; it might reveal profundities inimical to a way of life dependent on transient values, precariously concerned with immediate pleasures, and delicately adjusted to the cultivation of exquisite experience. There was peril in experience more robust.

Watteau

In spite of the shift away from Poussin's classicism, the art of the Coypels was still official. A certain contradiction is involved here. We would not expect to find the finest expression of intimate nuance in the work of academicians (including, later, Boucher) but in more introspective, more purely personal art. The painter who most perfectly summarized the new spirit in these terms was a man who died, in his middle thirties, a few years before Coypel painted *The Rape of Europa*. His name was Jean Antoine Watteau (1684-1721). Although his origins were ultimately Flemish, we think of him as a great painter in the French spirit that reached its climax in the eighteenth-century world of elegance, wit, and sophistication, tempered by sensitivity; his *Embarkation for Cythera* (Plate G2) has no close rival as the summation of this spirit, unless it is some other Watteau painting.

The Embarkation was Watteau's diploma picture, the work that every candidate for election to the Academy was required to submit. Watteau, who seems not to have been particularly interested in this official honor, probably painted *The Embarkation*, after long delays, only as a courtesy to his friends. He was never an official painter in spirit. His canvases were small and reticent; his patrons were private collectors of great discrimination rather than those who commissioned works for public or semipublic display. He would have been completely out of his element as director of the Academy in Rome.

As a student he had competed, unsuccessfully, for the Grand Prix de Rome, a prize that sent the winner to the Academy for several years under the sponsorship of the state. Watteau needed the prize badly; he had no financial means whatsoever. Years of privation intervened between his failure to win the Prix and the discovery of his talents by art collectors. Then he was comfortable for the rest of his life, but hardship had undermined his health. He suffered from tuberculosis, from which he was dying even when he was painting at the height of his powers.

Painters were admitted to the Academy under any one of several classifications, as history painters, portrait painters, genre painters, and the like. Since Watteau's art fitted into no existing classification, a new one had to be invented for him; he was called a painter of *fêtes galantes*. *Galant* is an untranslatable word. The English "gallant" is only a pale approximation. *Galant*, descended from an ancient French verb meaning to rejoice, is associated with men who are attentive to women, who are affable and seek to please, who are correct in dress and conduct, who are of delicate sensibilities, particularly those having to do with the pursuit of love in its lighter forms. The word can be slightly derogatory, especially when it is applied to a woman. A *femme galante* has good enough social standing but too easy virtue; a *vert galant* is a man well beyond first youth who continues to pursue women. Thus Watteau's *fêtes galantes*, including *The Embarkation for Cythera* (the island of Venus), are pictures of gatherings dedicated to the preliminary maneuvers and intrigues of seduction.

The subject, which could and frequently did lend itself to a licentious and cynical approach, received its most callous treatment toward the end of the century in a novel, *Les Liaisons dangereuses*, by Laclos, but in Watteau the

Alinari

Figure 4

theme is poetic. He seems to represent less than life-size characters in a less than life-size world of parklike perfection. They are engaged in a ritual that is its own reason for being, divorced from all others. Their pursuit of love is not corollary to other pursuits, not an excitement or a release from other activities; it is a life in itself, a gentle one, with no extensions beyond the ones Watteau paints.

Again we may make a comparison with a Venetian, not Titian this time but Giorgione as we saw him in *The Concert* (Plate E4). And again the fullness of the Venetian harmonies is reduced in *The Embarkation for Cythera*, the opulence of the sensuous symphony is modified, the glorification of the world of the senses is less apparent and is subjected to the rituals of cultivated sentiment. Or, even closer to Watteau, there is Rubens' *Garden of Love* (*Figure 4*), painted in the artist's old age as a glorification of his beautiful young wife, whose portrait appears many times over in this painting. Watteau is the artistic heir of both Giorgione and Rubens—quite directly the descendant of the latter, but the society of Watteau's time insisted on an exquisite veneer of formal observances as a cover for the values that Rubens glorified more sumptuously.

What we know of an artist as a person sometimes leads us to read into his work things that are not actually there. We must be cautious that our awareness of Rubens' rich and vital life and Watteau's early poverty and consuming disease does not influence us too much. Yet the gentleness of Watteau's art and its poetry—two characteristics that are indubitably present—do seem tempered by sadness, by a nostalgia for things missed or soon to be

Figure 5

lost. Once noticed, this quality is a determining one. One writer has called Watteau the gardener's boy who watches the party from the other side of the fence. The gleam of satins in the half light of a shadowy park, whispered conversations seen but not heard, lovers divorced from past and present life as they move quietly in their world of gentle intrigue—all these in Watteau are seen as if from beyond a barrier of which we are hardly conscious because to pass it would be an unthinkable intrusion.

Like so much eighteenth-century art, Watteau's work again and again suggests the theater. In his case the resemblance is more than coincidental, for he reflects the *commedia dell' arte*, an Italian comedy form that had become traditional in France. Some of his paintings, like *Mezzetin* (*Figure 5*), portray actors in the costume of stock characters in this stylized theater, which Watteau knew at first hand through its performances and through working, during his lean days, with Claude Gillot (1673–1722), a scenery designer and a painter of modes and intrigues suggested by the comedians.

This theater, which could be bawdy and racy, was banned during the last dreary years of Louis XIV's reign. But it continued to operate under cover and, when the old king died and Orléans became regent, it burst forth with even greater popularity, along with everything else that was witty, bright, gay, skilled, and sometimes just a little off color. To say that Watteau purified this subject matter would be inaccurate; he poeticized it, thus raising it above the level of Gillot's genre painting, just as Giorgione had poeticized Venetian preoccupation with voluptuous pleasures.

Like the Coypels, Watteau rejected the tradition of Poussin for that of Rubens, modifying it as we have just seen, building on Rubens' tradition of color and movement. Watteau's influence was great; he was an initiator of the rococo style. The fact that Watteau's pictures were in private collections kept the originals from being widely known, but the sets of engraved copies commissioned by one of his patrons, Jean de Jullienne, were extremely popular.

Boucher, among others, executed some of these engravings, with an inevitable effect on his own style. But the Boucher paintings we have seen should be sufficient indication that this excellent workman reduced Watteau's charm to formula, his delicacy to a recipe for daintiness, his poetry to decoration. Boucher was, in short, the academician of the new style.

Fragonard

With Watteau as the first generation and Boucher as the second, the tradition reached its wittiest and gayest peak in Jean Honoré Fragonard (1732–1806) as the third. By all accounts and by the evidence of paintings like *The Love Letter* (*Figure 6*), Frago (as he was affectionately called and as he often signed himself) was as delightful a person as could be found in Paris. Although he was a facile painter, sometimes to the point of being a careless one, he could be and most of the time was impeccable. He studied for a while with Boucher and became his assistant. He frequently emulated Boucher's style in all its frilly charm but with none of its frequent suggestion of mechanical production. He won the Prix de Rome and found patrons everywhere in the world of high fashion and high living. When necessary, he could paint as pompously as any traditional academician; he did so in order to win the Prix de Rome and, later, a place in the Academy. But his natural bent as an artist and as a man was toward happy, effervescent wit.

One of his important commissions was for Madame du Barry, the kindly little prostitute who succeeded Madame de Pompadour as the king's official mistress. He executed a series of pictures for her pavilion at Louveciennes illustrating a romantic escapade in which two young lovers meet, court, and win one another (*Figure 7*). In all likelihood they were intended as an allegory, requested by Madame du Barry, of the courtship of the aging monarch and his new love. If so, these exquisite scenes could have a tongue-in-cheek flavor. (Fragonard painted many frankly prankish and often dubiously erotic pictures, particularly as illustrations for books of the same tone.) Nobody has ever discovered exactly why Madame du Barry rejected them—to the ultimate advantage of a country then about to engage in a revolution based on moral and political principles that were to destroy her world and Fragonard's. The rejected works found their way to the United States, the finest group of pictures of the kind that have survived.

Figure 6

Morals and Shepherds

The American Revolution of 1776 and the French Revolution of 1789 were inspired by ideals concerning the dignity of the common man, a standard of social morality that had little to do with the ideals that produced the rococo style. Yet the new philosophy was discussed, largely as a fashionable exercise, in rococo salons. The English novelists of the century, like Fielding and Richardson, acute social commentators and in the end moralists, quickly became known in France and were imitated there by Abbé Prévost. The French philosophers who had created an intellectual "age of reason" now began to proclaim the superiority of sentiment over intellect. The eminent novelist, critic, philosopher, and Encyclopedist Denis Diderot (1713–1784) grew rhapsodical over an early manifestation of this sentimental morality in the work of the painter Jean Baptiste Greuze (1725–1805).

The most revolutionary of all the philosophers, Jean Jacques Rousseau, promulgated his doctrine that man in a state of nature was good and that artificial society had corrupted this goodness. At the height of the rococo period he insisted that to escape corruption one must return to nature. His novels gave

Figure 7

tremendous impetus to the popularity of the new sentimental morality in the salons; his *Social Contract* inspired the political conceptions of certain revolutionists; his love of nature opened a new movement, romanticism, that was to flourish in the next century, and he had an immediate, if curious, effect on the artificial society he damned.

All Rousseau's ideas, taken seriously and put into practice, would have undermined the privileges and pleasures of the very people who discussed them as the current intellectual rage. Eighteenth-century France made a fatal attempt to accommodate idealistic premise and cynical practice, abstract idealism and practical expediency. Voltaire was a philosopher with great respect for personal conscience and individual liberty; he was also the author of *Candide*, a devastating satire on philosophical premises that fail to see the world as it is, a place where innocence and natural nobility are, to say the least, impractical. The new morality, in the world it threatened, became another escape from boredom, a fad that offered conversationalists diverting gambits and gave painters new subjects.

Even Boucher capitalized on the taste for nature and simple things. In *The Dispatch of the Messenger* (Plate G 3), one of a series of four "pastoral" subjects, a shepherd dispatches a pigeon carrying a love letter to a shepherdess. The other episodes show the arrival of the pigeon, the shepherdess confiding in a friend, and finally the rendezvous of the lovers, the whole affair becoming the usual story of amorous intrigue, this time in peasant costumes. *The Dispatch of the Messenger* is an enchanting valentine; it is certainly not a philosophical document on the natural nobility of shepherds or the new social consciousness. Boucher's "rustic" scenes, like *The Interrupted Sleep* (*Figure 8*), with their barefooted and beribboned shepherdesses in pastoral settings, are variations of Watteau's *fêtes galantes*. They are conceived in the same spirit that led Marie Antoinette to build her

Figure 8

famous "mill" and to play shepherdess or milkmaid at parties whose cost would have supported a genuine shepherdess or milkmaid for life.

The most pretentious and artificial of the "moralist" painters was Greuze, whom Diderot, incredibly, called "true to nature." The description is applicable only insofar as Greuze painted simple village people in more realistic detail than Boucher. In elaborated genre pictures he told stories of ungrateful children and anguished parents, of repentant sons at the bedsides of dying fathers.

He is least pretentious in pictures like *Broken Eggs* (Plate G 4), which does exactly what Diderot said a picture should do: it teaches a moral lesson through the naturalistic presentation of an incident. In *Broken Eggs* we see, initially, a pure genre scene, not far from the Dutch and Flemish tradition of the preceding century. A farm girl or servant girl sits dejectedly beside an overturned basket of eggs, while an old woman scolds the young man who upset it. A little boy tries to mend one of the broken eggs, abandoning the bow and arrow with which he has been playing.

The bow and arrow are the clue to the moral

Alinari *Figure 9*

lesson; the child is a ragamuffin substitute for Cupid; the young man, we deduce from these hints, has brought the girl to a misfortune as irremediable as the breaking of an egg. Depending on one's point of view, the picture gains or loses in comparison with its earlier genre counterparts like De Hooch's *Interior* (Portfolio F, *Figure 25*). By Diderot's standard, it gains because it serves more than an esthetic function. By most standards today, it loses because the moralistic charade infringes on the abstract beauties that, in the long run, make a painting like the De Hooch more rewarding. The picture's moral lesson is certainly less interesting as such than as a reflection of the taste of the eighteenth century.

Greuze's best-known painting is *The Broken Pitcher* (*Figure 9*), one of his many sentimental allegories of dewy-eyed young girls marked by a false innocence that often masks a display of their charms, casually exposed by garments in disarray. In *The Broken Pitcher* Greuze is at his highest level of taste in this combination of surface innocence and seductive prettiness. (He was, on the other hand, an excellent portraitist.) The allegory, or moral, is the same as in *Broken Eggs*, with the symbol changed from eggs to a pitcher. Madame du Barry loved this picture so much that she purchased it herself.

Chardin

But if fashionable painters falsely reflected the new ideas of morality and the dignity of man, these concepts, passionately held by eighteenth-century thinkers, would be decisive in the struggles at the end of the century between the traditions of the Renaissance and the principles that were to govern the modern world. The new ideas were not only in the minds of philosophers; they were in the air. Their expression in art did not always take the incongruous form we have seen in Boucher and Greuze. The great exception is the work of Jean Baptiste Siméon Chardin (1699–1779), a good bourgeois generally classified as a painter of still life and genre. In both categories he came closer than any other artist of the century to presenting the new ideals in abstract form.

Chardin, a great painter and an honest man, did not illustrate these ideals in allegories, as Greuze did. Rather, when he painted an arrangement of a kitchen vessel with a few fruits and vegetables, he revealed the dignity that exists in simple things, giving them all the significance of great natural monuments. His *Self-Portrait* (*Figure 10*) shows us a plain, solid, intelligent face remindful of Benjamin Franklin. It hardly corresponds to the distorted idea of the typical eighteenth-century Frenchman we get from most painting of the time.

Chardin was a sound professional artist who sensibly turned his hand to whatever work came his way. He was a member of the Academy of Saint Luke, one of the secondary organizations descended from the medieval guilds, membership in which gave a painter professional standing without the kudos of belonging to the Royal Academy. He made his reputation in small exhibitions. He was elected to the Academy when Nicolas de Largillière (1656–1746), who did portraits of members of the court and the wealthy middle class, was attracted to his work. Largillière, a Frenchman raised in Antwerp, had worked in England under Sir Peter Lely, a painter in the Flemish tradition.

It was the "Flemish" quality of Chardin's work that pleased Largillière. Chardin now became popular as a painter of still life and genre in the tradition of the Low Countries, which had maintained its vogue in the eighteenth century. His work never sold for high prices, and there is no evidence that anyone recognized the truly exceptional way in which he invested ordinary subject matter with calm and dignified reality. Technical dexterity and picturesqueness accounted for the popularity of most still life and genre. Chardin's pictures are superior to the rank and file even on these grounds, but they are also great expressions of the human spirit filled with a deep, sober, unsentimental love of the honest and simple.

Alinari *Figure 10*

We saw in our preceding discussion that the Le Nains represented picturesque scenes from simple life with something of the same kind of understanding. Their *Procession of the Ram* (Plate F12) dignified a peasant festival by giving its participants an almost sculpturesque definition. Chardin does the same thing in pictures like *The Housekeeper* (Plate G5), but less obviously. He is closer to fundamental truths because, while we are conscious that the Le Nains impose dignity on a subject, Chardin convinces us that this dignity is inherent. It does not occur to us to doubt it. In Chardin's art the nobility of simple things is so undeniable that he can stand alone in France as the representative of this aspect of eighteenth-century thought and hold his own against the numerous artists who served an opposite ideal.

Outside France: Venice

For convenience we have spoken of the eighteenth century as if it hardly existed outside France. We must see now what has been happening in Italy, England, and America. About Italy there is little to add to what has been said here and in previous discussions of Italy's great past. But in Venice there was a late flowering that must be touched on briefly. We have already seen a representative example (*Figure 3*) of the work of the greatest Venetian rococo decorator, Giovanni Battista Tiepolo (1696–1770), who also worked in Spain and Germany.

Venice was entering a period of decay that would eventually make the city one vast romantic monument. In the eighteenth century there was enough inherited wealth to sustain for a few a life of fashionable elegance; for them there was pleasure and intrigue against an unmatched backdrop of water, air, light, and carved stone.

Canaletto (Antonio Canale, 1697–1768) and the painters of his workshop left hundreds of views of the inexhaustibly lovely city, drawn in sharply detailed perspective (*Figure 11*).

Figure 11

The work of his pupil Francesco Guardi (1712–1793) is even more evocative of the shimmering color and the casual pageantry of life in Venice, portrayed against the city's disintegrating monuments, as is so pleasantly demonstrated in his *Piazza San Marco, Venice* (Plate G6). Guardi abandoned the precise architectural definition of his teacher for rich, broken brushwork that anticipates the technique of the impressionists, a technique that plays its part in his constant suggestion of crumbling stone and forms impregnated with air and moisture and soft light.

It was not in character for Venice to produce a moralist, even a specious one like Greuze. She produced instead Pietro Longhi (1702–1785), who observed and recorded the life of social decadence with great liveliness. Longhi must be called a genre painter, although the subject matter in his city was almost bizarre enough to make him a painter of fantasy, especially when he painted scenes of the carnivals (*Figure 12*) with which the Venetians entertained themselves in the twilight of their greatness.

English Portraits

In England it was another story. The country prospered above all others in Europe, and, although it was not invariably blessed in its monarchs, it was usually fortunate in its statesmen. It had never had a Versailles to reduce its aristocracy to impotence and parasitism and bleed its middle class, which became affluent. The luxurious life of its great houses was supported by wealth acquired by hardheaded policy and a merchant fleet that brought wealth from all over the world. There had never been a thoroughgoing rococo style in England, in spite of the fantasies of Chippendale and others. Even at its most elaborate, English life and style retained its traditional sturdiness.

English painting had long been dominated by imported artists—Holbein, Van Dyck, and Lely among them. England's Royal Academy, marking the coming of age of a national school of painting, was formed only in 1768, over a century after its French counterpart. Its first president, who was knighted at the time of his installation, was Sir Joshua Reynolds (1723–1792), a good conservative painter who gave the Academy a good conservative character, based on rules and regulations respectful to the old masters.

Reynolds fancied himself a painter in the grand manner and turned out numerous pictures influenced by the late renaissance and baroque Italians, whom he admired. He was a sound painter who could be a stuffy one. He could present a startling projection of personality if his sitter did so, as did Samuel Johnson (*Figure 13*). At its worst Reynolds' art was pompous, flatulent, or mawkish; at his typical best he reflected, in portraits of the gentry, the English eighteenth-century virtues of dignified manner and solid practicality, as he did in *The Honorable Henry Fane* (Plate G 7).

Reynolds' position as England's foremost artist, which he industriously nurtured, was threatened by only one man, Thomas Gainsborough (1727–1788), a born painter who took London by storm following a career in the

Figure 12

Reproduced by courtesy of the Trustees of the Tate Gallery, London

Figure 13

fashionable city of Bath and the country houses near it. Reynolds was a conscientious painter; Gainsborough was a brilliant, fluent one. Reynolds was an ambitious man who worked hard for his success; Gainsborough a natural charmer whose personality, like his painting, recalls Watteau and Fragonard.

It is impossible to write for long about Gainsborough without referring to *Jonathan Buttall: The Blue Boy* (*Figure 14*), which by legend was painted to challenge Reynolds' contention that blue could not be used as the dominant tone of a painting. Legend aside, Gainsborough proved in *The Blue Boy* and in numerous other "blue" pictures that as a colorist he outshone Reynolds. Working within a strictly limited palette, Gainsborough could paint a picture of rich color interest, while Reynolds could run the gamut and, as often as not, turn up with a pleasant but obvious combination of tints.

Gainsborough had little interest in the character of his subjects; the charm of the people he paints is Gainsborough's own charm relayed through the image of another person.

Figure 14

The enchanting *Mary, Countess Howe* (Plate G8) is Gainsborough at his most entrancing. It is one of the most delightfully painted pictures of any century, exactly the kind that maddened Reynolds because it seemed effortless, was irresistibly attractive, and yet was undeniably a great painting in the tradition of Rubens and Van Dyck. In a fit of pique Reynolds called Gainsborough "the greatest landscape painter of Europe," an unsuccessful and heavy-handed effort to damn Gainsborough's portraits by praising their backgrounds.

English Landscape

Gainsborough, in fact, regarded his portraits as a way to make a living. He much preferred doing landscapes—or playing his viola da gamba—to this profitable work. No painter before him had so captured the feel of the countryside with its soft air, springy turf, purling flow of water and fresh, delicately foliaged trees, the fleeciness of scudding clouds, the cool depths of shade, and the happy union of boatmen, strollers, and farmers in this natural Elysium (*Figure 15*).

In spite of its technical connections with Dutch painting, Gainsborough's Elysium is already thoroughly English in spirit, with the Englishness that was on the point of receiving expression in the art of pure landscapists and the nature poets. In France, Rousseau based his theory of nature and of man's nobility within it on speculations as to the constituting factors of this creature man, and French painters first investigated landscape under the influence of these ideas. But in England the response to nature was spontaneous, born of participation in its pleasures and without resort to theory.

Gainsborough cannot claim the parentage of English landscape. That title belongs to his somewhat older contemporary, Richard Wilson (1714–1782). What we know of Wilson is incomplete and contradictory. He was certainly well considered at the time of the organization of the Royal Academy, for he was one of the founding members. But his patrons had a way of dropping him—or he them—and apparently he was obscure during much of his life. He worked for a time in Italy. There, and later in England, he did classical landscapes in the tradition of Poussin and Claude Lorrain, modified by romantic interest in ruins and picturesque locales. The increasingly quiet and unpretentious character of Wilson's work leaves us with the feeling that here was a man who kept to himself. He turned more and more away from synthetic classical landscapes and toward scenes that were true to nature. Other painters before him had done so, notably in the Low Countries, but Wilson differed from them by discovering in the most ordinary stretch of field and sky all the poetic mood that most landscapists created by selecting picturesque or extraordinary subjects. He differs from Gainsborough in an important way. A

Gainsborough landscape may be idyllic but that quality is generalized and hence a step removed from the intimate response stirred by one of Wilson's naturalistic, yet perceptive, scenes.

On Hounslow Heath (Plate G9) includes no exceptional elements. It seems to be painted rather literally—certainly with respect for the actual topography. But it is like a portrait that respects the features of the sitter and reproduces them quite closely, yet somehow manages to offer us more than a surface account, telling us of the personality of the subject and of the painter's own reaction to it. Hounslow Heath would not make a very effective snapshot; it is an uneventful stretch of open ground. But Wilson gives us all the quality of a delightful day and a delightful place, the kind of impression we would like to fix in our mind as a record of a place and a time in which we felt a particularly affecting communion with fields, streams, and low hills. This is Wilson's great talent, his ability to reveal the poetry in the unexceptional (a talent comparable in its way to Chardin's), and it is his just claim to the fatherhood of an English landscape tradition.

England: Fantasy and Morality

England produced the supreme visionary and, contrastingly, the most trenchant social moralist among eighteenth-century artists.

The visionary was William Blake (1757–1827), so individual an artist that there is no reason for trying to relate him either to the eighteenth or the nineteenth century (his work having been divided by the year 1800) except that chronologically he belongs to both. Since

Figure 15

Figure 16

we have already spoken of Blake in detail (Portfolio 5, *Figure 10*, and Portfolio 12, Plate 134), we will give only a single reminder of the rhythmic linear schemes in which he recorded his visions, including those inspired by the book of Job and *The Divine Comedy* (*Figure 16*).

We have also said a great deal about William Hogarth (1697–1764) in discussing *A Rake's Progress* (Portfolio 11, Plate 129 and *Figures 15–21*). No other painter contrasts more strongly with Blake. Hogarth was as worldly as Blake was visionary. Blake recorded visions of the Inferno and Paradise whereas Hogarth set down a detailed record of low life and high life in the London about him. Blake and Hogarth, however, had one thing in common: each carried on a lifelong feud with the painting standards of the day, Blake in his fulminations against Reynolds, whom he called "Sir Sloshua," and Hogarth in his contempt for the affectations of art dilettantes. Hogarth's portraits, like the one of his sister (*Figure 17*), are incisive records of features and character, awarding justice where justice is due but never mercy where it would be a professional concession. It is easy to see why he received fewer commissions than inferior painters who had a knack for capturing an adequate likeness and, at the same time, for flattering the sitter.

As a moralist, in *A Rake's Progress* and in his other narrative series, Hogarth is anything but sentimental. The fourth episode from *Marriage à la Mode* (*Figure 18*) includes in its multitude of details the opening maneuvers in the seduction by a young man about town of a young wife, the victim of a loveless marriage. When we oppose the atmosphere of this episode to Watteau's light treatment of such affairs, we are at two poles of the interpretation of amorous intrigue, so far apart that there is actually no relationship between the pictures. And we need hardly comment on Hogarth's difference from Greuze.

Even in England Hogarth was alone in the directness and honesty of his comments on society. The engraved versions of his moral tales were extremely popular, but more for their lively narrative than for their social comment. They remain popular today for the same reason, and because time has made picturesque the places and costumes that were literal records of the contemporary world when Hogarth painted them.

Two generations after Hogarth, the painter George Morland (1763–1804) was successful with moral comments that bowed deeply to the public's taste for Rousseauism and that showed the rewards of conventional virtue. He painted happy farmers in rustic settings or reassuring subjects like the *Fruits of Early Industry and Economy* (*Figure 19*), showing a bourgeois surrounded by his children and grandchildren, who have called on him at his office. Through

Reproduced by courtesy of the Trustees of the Tate Gallery, London

Figure 17

the window we see a busy port crowded with his barges and warehouses. He has a black servant (a mark of caste) and a country house, pictured on the wall. In spite of his success he is still conscientious in small matters: his respectful clerk, ledger in hand, quill pen in mouth, is counting out coins into his palm.

The Americans

Life in colonial America in the eighteenth century ranged from an extreme simplicity enforced by circumstance to a reasonable approximation of the good life of the mother country, England. We can say the same of the American painting of the time, remembering that neither in life nor in art was there a parallel to the extreme aristocratic sophistication that produced Gainsborough.

In the simplest and most purely American tradition there were the "limners," painters with little if any formal training who traveled from place to place picking up work in communities that could not support an artist full time. Among other things, they did signboards (an eighteenth-century signboard was no mean affair; both Watteau and Chardin did famous ones), but these have largely disappeared. We remember the limners best for their portraits. Some are merely quaint; others need no apologies as works of art.

The work of an untaught, or "primitive," painter is likely to be rigidly drawn and brightly colored, with emphasis on precisely delineated details, all typified by a paradoxical effort toward exact representation combined with faulty perspective and proportion. These are the marks of the amateur, but they are not limitations that need stifle talent, especially when there is a feeling for line and flat pattern. In *The De Peyster Boy with a Deer* (*Figure 20*) the line of the deer's muzzle, neck, and leg show that this anonymous limner was an artist. Other parts of the picture further prove it—the inner curve of the boy's open coat (echoed by the curves of the bench behind

Figure 18

him and the ornamental ledge between the deer's feet), the contrasting severe vertical lines in the upper right quarter, the pleasant variety of the landscape (as flat as a scenic backdrop), and the nice placement of ornamental shapes.

In rebuttal we might argue that the landscape "backdrop" is not effectively realistic, as the painter probably would have liked it to be, or decorative in the same way as the rest of the picture. Also, the strong line between the architecture and the landscape may divide too emphatically too near the exact center of the picture, slicing with disconcerting conspicuousness through the boy's head. And certainly no one can pretend that the deer's front legs are accurately drawn. Yet these inconsistencies and awkwardnesses are part of the appealing character of the picture, which speaks of a society in which graces were cultivated against a background of limitations. In this sense *The De Peyster Boy* is not a second-rate English painting but a first-rate American one.

Nevertheless, this Americanism was the result of circumstance rather than intention. Every artist who could do so studied in England and tried to approximate the English style. An unhappy example is Ralph Earl (1751–1801), whose early portraits, like the famous *Roger Sherman* (*Figure 21*), preserved the essence of the eighteenth-century New Englander in his alertness, practicality, and sobriety. But Earl went to London, studied there, became a member of the Royal Academy, and returned to America with a bag of tricks that made him a more conventionally skilled painter but a less forthright one. The vigorous, rather harsh naïveté of his style had been sacrificed to an ill-digested sophistication.

Boston and Philadelphia, the largest and most prosperous colonial cities, offered the closest approximation to the English way of life, with their mansions, theaters, and fine public buildings, their busy ports and international visitors. And, naturally, they produced or attracted the most skilled craftsmen and artists.

In Boston, John Singleton Copley (1737–1815) became established as the outstanding colonial painter, a reputation he deserved and still holds. His stepfather, an English engraver, must have taught the boy something of drawing, but Copley, like other Americans, had to learn by studying whatever painting and prints were at hand and by training himself. At fifteen he was already producing respectable work, and he ultimately became an expert realist with a tight, meticulous manner saved from dryness by the straightforward veracity with which he represented his sitters, by his startling reproduction of the textures and colors of their clothing, furniture, and objects, and by the beautifully smooth and glossy surface of his paint, all evident in *Mrs. Seymour Fort* (Plate G10). Like the work of less expert painters, including Earl, Copley's art was marked as American by its lack of fluency; yet to call this a "lack" is to miss the vigorous spirit and the expert craftsmanship that more than atoned for Copley's limitations in comparison with the best English artists.

Copley himself, however, felt restive under these limitations. Yearning for a larger world, he sent a painting to London where it was exhibited and praised. Just before the American Revolution he made a long-desired trip to England and Italy. Still an exact worker, he managed to acquire some of the grace his European contemporaries achieved in their painting. But it was not in his nature as an artist, or in his experience as a person, to work in the sophisticated manner that became increasingly popular in England. He spent the rest of his life there, his Tory family having emigrated to London, but his success was limited. The great American ended his life as a second-string Englishman.

A Philadelphian, Benjamin West (1738–1820), was more fortunate. Like Copley, a prodigy, he was only twenty-two when a group of patrons sent him to Europe. As a handsome exotic who claimed that his first painting lessons came from the Indians who taught him how they made their colors, West became the rage of Italian society. He repeated his success in England, where he spent the rest of his long life, becoming a court painter and president of the Royal Academy. Streams of young Americans came to his studio, studied with him, and returned to the United States to Europeanize the local traditions.

One of West's students, briefly and before the Revolution, was Charles Willson Peale

Figure 19

Courtesy of the New-York Historical Society, New York City *Figure 20*

(1741–1827), an extraordinary man who found time to paint along with other activities that included saddlery, coachmaking, watchmaking, silversmithing, dentistry, taxidermy, and museum organization and direction. As if these hobbies, trades, and professions were not enough, he was active in government and in the affairs of the Revolution, being a member of the General Assembly and an officer in Washington's army.

Whatever Peale absorbed under West's instruction is less apparent in his painting than is the tradition of Copley, whom he had once gone to Boston to watch at work. Even more than Copley's, his American portraits suggest the shrewd and sincere, if at times awkward, character of the colonists and the citizens of the new nation. He was an uneven painter, but his *Staircase Group* (Plate G11) has strong claims as the finest American portrait of its time, along with the best of Copley's. Painted exactly life size, it originally hung on a wall inside the frame of an actual doorway, with a real step leading to the painted ones. The device was in character with Peale's love of experiment and his direct and unanalytical conviction that the first job of painting was to create an illusion of reality. The illusion in *Staircase Group*, even without the frame and the step, is startling. (George Washington, on a visit to Peale, is supposed to have doffed his hat politely to the two young men on the staircase, a likely story.) The beauty of the picture lies in its harmonious tonality, in the modulations of light and shadow, and in the affectionate observation of the models, who were two of the artist's sons. These factors may be largely inherent in the picture's realism, but by concentrating on them Peale raised *The Staircase Group* above the level of a tour-de-force.

Peale was the founder of a dynasty of American artists. His *Peale Family* (Portfolio 7, Plate 74) shows him with his brothers, whom he taught to paint. His eleven children were all named after artists he admired.

This interesting man was the individual most responsible for the founding of America's

Courtesy of Yale University Art Gallery *Figure 21*

Figure 22

first art school, the Pennsylvania Academy of the Fine Arts, which still flourishes. Restless, inventive, zealous, exuberant, full of youthful curiosity to the end of his life, Peale was a man of his century in his interest in science. For the last forty years of his life he was preoccupied with a museum of natural history. (When he could not find actual objects for the collection, he painted them.) His *Exhuming the First American Mastodon* (*Figure 22*) is an exceptional early American painting, recording one of his more spectacular undertakings.

David: the End of an Epoch

While painting followed a generally placid course on the other side of the Channel and across the Atlantic, art in France was subjected to an eruptive force that shattered the old traditions and began the series of revolutions and counter-revolutions that dominate the art history of our time. This force was personified in Jacques Louis David (1748–1825), whose revolution in painting occurred simultaneously, and not coincidentally, with the French Revolution itself. David's *Brutus* (Plate G12), exhibited in 1789, the very year the Revolution began, was greeted as a call to arms, for reasons that we will see. David was one of the talented students who received, through the patronage of the king, annual stipends to follow their studies at the Academy's school. (Often the students were quartered in the Louvre, which was not yet officially a museum.) After four successive failures to win the Prix de Rome, he attempted suicide. He was saved by fellow students and in the next competition he won the Prix with an elaborate picture that followed, respectfully and obediently, the current academic recipes for rococo style.

A reaction against the excesses of rococo, however, was current even within that style. The indomitably classical spirit of France was coming to the surface again, given impetus by the sensational excavations of the buried cities of Pompeii and Herculaneum. They yielded a multitude of new objects for study and corrected men's ideas of the ancient past by bringing them closer than before to the life of those times. Madame de Pompadour sponsored new, straight-lined, semiclassical designs in furniture and interiors that have come to be called the Louis XVI style. Among painters there was a vogue for classical subjects, although, in truth, they had little to do with the classical spirit. David left for his studies in Rome declaring that he would not yield to classicism. Once there, in the presence of the ancient monuments, he about-faced, saying that the sight of them had removed scales from his eyes.

The exhibition in Paris of his first completely classical picture, *The Oath of the Horatii* (*Figure 23*), was a decisive turning point in the history of art. It created the kind of excitement that is possible only in France, a country where art is debated as fervently as politics and is so much a part of national life that the exhibition of a picture or the presentation of a drama may affect the standing of the government. David's reaction against rococo affectations had gone far beyond the picturesque classicism of his contemporaries, beyond the ornamental adaptations of the Louis XVI style, even beyond the sedateness of Poussin, the classical demigod. In *The Oath of the Horatii*, his economically, even bitterly, disciplined composition shows a Roman father receiving his sons' pledge to return from battle victorious or to die on the field, while the women of the household grieve in the restrained manner befitting the wives and sisters and sweethearts of heroes dedicated to the honor of their country. *The Oath of the Horatii* received a riotous reception. Esthetically it rejected the sweetness and feminine grace that had dominated painting for three generations; ideologically it rejected amorous lightness or specious sentiment for moral force. Most sensational of all, politically it was interpreted by burgeoning revolutionary elements as an antiroyalist allegory, promoting the virility of the new ideals against the degeneracy of the old regime.

David followed *The Oath of the Horatii* with other "stoic" pictures on the general theme of self-sacrifice to moral and political principles. We have seen one of them, *The Death of Socrates* (Portfolio 11, Plate 126), in another discussion. The last of the series was the *Brutus*, whose exhibition coincided with the outbreak of the Revolution.

The picture shows Brutus, who, as First Consul of Rome, had condemned his own sons to death, as their bodies are brought home to him. Whether or not David intended a direct inference, the subject was interpreted as a criticism of Louis XVI, who had allowed members of his own family to emigrate and take up arms against France instead of condemning them as traitors. The comparison between Brutus' courage and Louis's weakness was openly made; David's painting was called a challenge to all Frenchmen to purify France at whatever cost, at whatever sacrifice. Like *The Oath of the Horatii* and *The Death of Socrates*, it was painted with an icy, unyielding precision appropriate to the rigid self-control of Brutus; technically and emotionally it allowed no quarter to frilly charm or sentimentality.

In politics and in painting, the old regime was doomed. Never has there been a closer parallel between art and current events, never a more significant connection between the two, and never, certainly, a more deliberately cal-

Alinari

Figure 23

culated disruption of established standards. The student who had been denied the Prix de Rome for so long, who had maintained an antipathy toward the Academy even after winning it, now became art dictator of France and a power in the revolutionary government. He was a member of the body that voted the death of his former patron, the pathetic king, and he abolished the Academy, its schools, and its tradition. But the new autocracy, following David's formulas, was more rigid than the one it replaced. David, in effect, created the first dictatorship in art. The results of his acts will occupy us in our next several discussions.

Color Plates

Figures in the Text

18. MARRIAGE À LA MODE: IV, THE TOILET, by William Hogarth (1697–1764), British

Engraving. Height 22″. The Metropolitan Museum of Art, Dick Fund, 1932

19. FRUITS OF EARLY INDUSTRY AND ECONOMY, by George Morland (1763–1804), British

Oil on canvas. Height 30¼″. The Philadelphia Museum of Art

20. THE DE PEYSTER BOY WITH A DEER, by an unknown artist (active 1720s and 1730s), American

Oil on canvas. Height 50¼″. The New-York Historical Society

21. ROGER SHERMAN, by Ralph Earl (1751–1801), American

Oil on canvas. Height 5′ 4⅝″. Yale University Art Gallery, New Haven

22. EXHUMING THE FIRST AMERICAN MASTODON, 1806–08, by Charles Willson Peale (1741–1827), American

Oil on canvas. Height 50″. The Peale Museum, Baltimore, gift of Mrs. Harry White

23. THE OATH OF THE HORATII, 1784, by Jacques Louis David (1748–1825), French

Oil on canvas. Height 10′ 9¾″. The Louvre Museum, Paris